over the Top!

Norzailina Nordin

Marshall Cavendish Cuisine

© 2004 Marshall Cavendish International (Asia) Private Limited

Published by Marshall Cavendish Cuisine
An imprint of Marshall Cavendish International (Asia) Private Limited
A member of Times Publishing Limited
Times Centre, 1 New Industrial Road, Singapore 536196
Tel: (65) 6213 9288   Fax: (65) 6285 4871
E-mail: te@sg.marshallcavendish.com
Online Bookstore: www.marshallcavendish.com/genref

Malaysian Office:
Federal Publications Sdn Berhad (General & Reference Publishing) (3024-D)
Times Subang, Lot 46, Persiaran Teknologi Subang
Subang Hi-Tech Industrial Park
Batu Tiga, 40000 Shah Alam
Selangor Darul Ehsan, Malaysia
Tel: (603) 5635 2191   Fax: (603) 5635 2706
E-mail: cchong@tpg.com.my

National Library Board (Singapore) Cataloguing in Publication Data

Norzailina Nordin.
Over the top! / Norzailina Nordin. – Singapore : Marshall Cavendish Cuisine, c2004.
p. cm.
ISBN : 981-232-450-X

1. Cake decorating. I. Title.

TX771.2
641.8653 — dc21   SLS2004049512

Printed in Singapore by Saik Wah Press Pte Ltd

The publisher wishes to thank
Remix Home Shoppe Sdn Bhd and
Royel Department Store for the loan and use of their tableware.

Editor: Lydia Leong

Designer: Lynn Chin Nyuk Ling

Photographer: Jenhor Siow

Dedication

To all potential and professional cake decorators searching for ideas,
or just anyone who loves to see a prettily decorated cake—
here is a book that will fulfil your every whim and desire.

Contents

Preface   7

Acknowledgements   9

Come and Celebrate

Cherry Blossoms   12

Fire Crackers   15

New Year Cheer   16

Ketupat Wishes   19

Blue Mosque   20

Colourful Kolam   23

Graduation Day   24

Tier of Roses   27

Congratulations   28

Love Always

Here is my Heart   32

Strawberry Surprise   35

Queen of Hearts   36

Luxurious Chocolate   39

Roses in the Box   40

Box of Chocolates   43

Iced Rosies   44

Christmas Joy

Basket of Poinsettias   48

Stocking of Gifts   51

Gifts   52

Fancy Candles   55

Snowman   56

Fir Tree   59

Christmas on a Hill   60

Special Occasions

Specially for the Children

Space Rocket 64

Train of Goodies 67

Cars on the Road 68

Fish in a Dish 71

Colourful Butterfly 72

Pink Princess 75

Tea Party 76

Hedgehog 79

Erupting Volcano 80

Zoo Trip 84

Dip in the Pool 87

Boat on a Lake 88

Loving Football 91

Tunnel and Train 92

Snakes and Ladders 95

Green Monster 96

Horror Sorcerer 99

Treasure Chest 100

Tutty Fruity 104

Carrot Heart 107

Springtime Flowers 108

Hat of Blossoms 111

Bowl of Eggs 112

Happy Gardening 115

Stack of Books 116

Pineapple Delight 119

Laces and Beads 120

Techniques and Templates 123

Basic Recipes 139

Mixing Colours 157

Equipment 158

Weights and Measures 160

Preface

Back in 1980, at the age of 18, I received a prize from my school, Methodist Girls' Secondary, for achieving the highest score in one of my subjects, Bahasa Malaysia (Malay language). The teachers back then knew that I was also a keen student in Home Sciences and thus they decided to give me a cookbook as my prize! And guess what the title was? *Creative Cake Decorating* by Rose Cantrell, 1978.

Who would have thought, that after almost 24 years, I would come up with my own cake decoration book, *Over The Top!*?

I am very happy for this opportunity to be able to do this book. I may not have graduated in a course on cake decorating from an established academy of baking, but that only proves that you need not be schooled in the art of cake decorating in order to make a cake look pretty. You only need to know the basics, and the rest is quite 'easy'. Just don't give up, as cake decorating is a craft that requires a lot of patience and perseverance.

Over the Top! is not entirely a cookbook on cake decoration, and neither is it 'just another cake decorating book'. It is, instead, a cookbook that was written to fire your imagination as you browse through its colourful pages. These are just some basic ideas for you to use as a springboard to even more personalised and special cakes.

May you find each cake featured here an inspiration. And may you enjoy endless hours of excitement working with the many, many types of icings!

Norzailina Nordin
September 2004

7

Acknowledgements

I thank my family for their support, my friends for their encouragement, and David and Jamilah from Marshall Cavendish International (Asia) for their confidence in me.

I would also like to express my thanks to Kedai Kek Mona, Bake Oven, Bakewell and Chef Mohd Anuar Draman.

Thanks also to Noorhasimah Tahrim for her assistance during the photoshoot preparation and to Nazratul Waheeda Nadzri and Terry J.

My utmost gratitude goes to another two members from Marshall Cavendish International (Asia)—Lynn, for her cheerfulness despite the endless hard work, and Lydia for her meticulous editing. I also extend my thanks to the team from Jen Studio who was most helpful in keeping our spirits high during the long photography sessions. *Over the Top!* is truly a result of hours of hard work and thus a wonderful achievement for us all!

Come
and
Celebrate

Cherry Blossoms

1

2

3

Cake and Decoration

15 cm square cake	1
Butter icing	100 g
Hot apricot glaze	40 g
Dark pink fondant	900 g, rolled out into a thin sheet
Pink fondant	125 g, rolled out into a thin sheet
Semi-sweet cooking chocolate	100 g, finely chopped
Vegetable shortening	1 tsp
Royal icing	250 g
Red and yellow food colouring	

Equipment

1 cm round cookie cutter	1
Piping bags	4
Ruby FM 809 or No. 8 star tip	1

Method

1. Slice cake horizontally to get 2 square cake layers then sandwich with butter icing.

2. Spread apricot glaze all over cake and cover with dark pink fondant sheet. Place cake on a serving platter.

3. Cut circles from pink fondant sheet with a cookie cutter. Bring sides of each circle together to form a petal. Set aside.

4. Combine and melt chocolate and shortening in a bowl over a pan of simmering water. Remove from heat and cool slightly.

5. Fill a piping bag with cooled chocolate mixture. Snip off tip and pipe lines to represent trunk and branches of a cherry tree.

6. Mix 200 g of royal icing with a few drops of red colouring. Place in a piping bag fitted with a star tip. Pipe a row of stars around base of cake.

7. Divide remaining royal icing into 2 parts. Mix 1 portion with a few drops of yellow colouring. Place both portions into separate piping bags and snip off tips.

8. Form cherry blossoms on cake using 5 pink petals for each flower. Use white icing to secure their positions. Pipe yellow icing as centres of flowers.

9. Use remaining white royal icing to pipe 'Happy Chinese New Year' on cake. Use lettering template on pg 125 as a guide, if preferred.

Fire Crackers

1

2

5

Cake and Decoration

8 x 4 cm Swiss rolls	6
Hot apricot glaze	40 g
Dark red fondant	600 g, rolled out into a thin sheet
Black royal icing	70 g

Equipment

Thick black and gold string	1.2 m
Piping bag	1
No. 2 writing tip	1
20 cm square cake board	1

Method

1 Brush Swiss rolls with apricot glaze.

2 Cover them with dark red fondant.

3 Cut string into 6 equal lengths. Shape 1 length into a loop and secure with some thread.

4 Make a small hole at one end of each Swiss roll.

5 Insert ends of string into Swiss rolls to look like fire crackers. Attach loop to a Swiss roll to complete fire crackers.

6 Place black royal icing in a piping bag fitted with a writing tip. Pipe motifs on crackers. Set aside to dry.

7 Position fire crackers carefully onto cake board.

New Year Cheer

3

4

5

Cake and Decoration

20 cm round cake	1
Butter icing	160 g
Hot apricot glaze	40 g
Orange-red fondant	600 g, rolled out into a thin sheet
Brownish-green marzipan	220 g
Orange marzipan	100 g
Green and brown food colouring	
Yellow royal icing	50 g

Equipment

22 cm round cake board	1
Spoon/fork with decorative handle	1
Cocktail stick	1
Cloves	7
Piping bag	1
No. 2 writing tip	1

Method

1   Slice cake horizontally to get 2 round cake layers then sandwich with butter icing.

2   Place cake on cake board and brush with apricot glaze. Cover cake with orange-red fondant.

3   Trim off excess orange-red fondant and shape into a strip long enough to go around base of cake. Brush base of cake with a little water to secure strip. Press handle of spoon or fork on strip to make a pattern.

4   Shape brownish-green marzipan into bamboo stems and leaves. Secure onto top of cake with some water.

5   Shape orange marzipan into 7 small balls and flatten slightly to resemble mandarin oranges. Use a cocktail stick to mark tiny holes on each mandarin and complete look with a clove. Arrange on cake.

6   Spoon yellow royal icing into a piping bag fitted with a writing tip and pipe Chinese New Year greetings on cake. Use lettering template on pg 125 as a guide, if preferred.

Ketupat Wishes

1

5

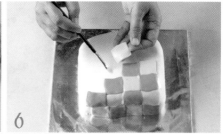

6

Cake and Decoration

15 cm square cake	1
Butter icing	100 g
Royal icing	250 g
White fondant	500 g, rolled out into a thin sheet
Light green fondant	800 g, rolled out into a thin sheet
Dark green fondant	300 g, rolled out into a thin sheet
Yellow sugar	60 g

Equipment

25 cm square cake board	1
Cake smoother	1

Method

1 Carefully trim corners of cake to make them rounded.

2 Slice cake horizontally to get 2 cake layers then sandwich with butter icing.

3 Place cake on cake board and spread royal icing over the top and sides of cake.

4 Cover cake with white fondant.

5 Cut out 33–35 squares each measuring 3 x 3 cm from light green fondant sheet. Repeat with dark green fondant sheet.

6 Brush cake with some water then make a chequered pattern on cake with fondant squares. When done, run over surface of cake with a cake smoother.

7 Roll remaining light green fondant into a 25 x 2 cm strip. Cut to get 2 strips, one 10 cm and the other 15 cm. Repeat with dark green fondant.

8 Moisten exposed areas of cake board with a little water. Spoon yellow sugar onto board around cake. Carefully lay green fondant strips at 2 opposite corners of cake to complete look of *ketupat*.

Blue Mosque

3

5

6

Cake and Decoration

15 cm square cake	1
Butter icing	300 g
Light blue fondant	1 kg, rolled out into a thin sheet
8 cm bowl-shaped cake	1
White royal icing	250 g
Black fondant	80 g, rolled out into a thin sheet

Equipment

25 cm square polystyrene board	1
Gold-coloured paper	1, sheet, 40 x 40 cm
20 cm square cake board	1
Dowel rods	3
Piping bags	2
Bakery crafts no. 98 or No. 7 shell tip	1
No. 2 writing tip	1
Cylindrical polystyrene tube	1, 20 x 3.5 cm
Crescent cut-out (see pg 126)	1

Method

1 Cut a 3.5 cm wide circle from a corner of polystyrene board so mosque tower can be inserted later. Cover polystyrene board with gold-coloured paper. Set aside.

2 Slice square cake horizontally to get 2 square cake layers then sandwich with some butter icing. Place cake onto cake board then spread with some remaining butter icing and cover with light blue fondant. Reserve remaining butter icing and light blue fondant.

3 Stick 3 dowel rods into square cake so they are equally spaced. Ensure they go through to cake board underneath. Make a small mark at the point at which they become level with the top of cake. Pull them out and trim to size. Re-insert trimmed rods into cake.

4 Spread remaining butter icing onto bowl-shaped cake. Roll out remaining light blue fondant and cover cake. Trim off any excess and reserve.

5 Smear about 2 Tbsp of royal icing over top of square cake and place bowl-shaped cake into position on top. Spoon remaining royal icing into a piping bag fitted with a shell tip and pipe shells around base of bowl-shaped cake.

6 Cut 16 doors from black fondant. Stick 4 doors on each side of square cake with water. Using a piping bag fitted with a writing tip, pipe pattern on doors with white royal icing. Pipe shells around base of square cake.

7 Spread remaining butter icing onto polystyrene tube and cover with light blue fondant to create mosque tower. Shape some fondant into a cone and stick to top of tower with some white royal icing.

8 Position cake onto polystyrene board and insert mosque tower in place. Place crescent on top of dome.

Colourful Kolam

1

4

6

Cake and Decoration

Royal icing	120 g
15 cm round cake	1
Butter icing	250 g
White fondant	450 g, rolled out into a thin sheet
Red, blue, yellow and green sugar	20–30 g each

Equipment

20 cm square glass sheet	1
Kolam template (see pg 127)	1
Piping bag	1
No. 2 writing tip	1
20 cm round cake board	1
2 cm wide gold ribbon	60 cm
4 cm wide silver ribbon	60 cm

Method

1 Place glass on *kolam* template and carefully pipe design with royal icing placed in a piping bag fitted with a writing tip. Allow to dry.

2 Slice cake horizontally to get 2 round cake layers then sandwich with some butter icing. Place on cake board.

3 Spread remaining butter icing over top and sides of cake.

4 Cover cake with white fondant. Press glass with dried *kolam* design onto fondant firmly so it leaves an impression.

5 Place royal icing into a piping bag fitted with a writing tip and pipe design using the impression as a guide. Allow to dry.

6 Spoon coloured sugar carefully to fill segments on design.

7 Tie gold and silver ribbon around base of cake, securing with a dot of royal icing.

23

Graduation Day

1

2

4

Cake and Decoration

Pale brown fondant	200 g, rolled out into a thin sheet
Hot apricot glaze	30 g
6 cm high cupcakes	6
Butter icing	250 g
Orange, black and brown food colouring	
Red fondant icing	1 Tbsp

Equipment

Piping bags	3
10 cm round doilies	6
0.5 cm wide ribbons, tied into bows	2
Gold dragees	4–6
Mortarboards (see pg 128)	6

Method

1. Cut out faces from pale brown fondant sheet.
2. Brush some apricot glaze onto one side of cupcakes and attach faces.
3. Take 2 Tbsp of butter icing, add some orange colouring and place into a piping bag. Divide remaining butter icing into 2 portions. Add a few drops of black colouring to 1 portion and brown to the other. Spoon into separate piping bags.
4. Snip tip off piping bag with black icing and pipe eyes on faces. Snip a larger hole and pipe short black hair for boys' heads on 3 cupcakes.
5. Snip tip of piping bag with brown icing and pipe lips for boys. Snip a larger hole and pipe long brown hair for girls' heads.
6. Shape red fondant icing as lips for girls. Use orange butter icing to pipe noses on faces.
7. Place heads on doilies and decorate girls' hair with ribbons and use dragees as earrings. Press mortarboards lightly onto heads.

Tier of Roses

2

3

5

Cake and Decoration

25 cm round cake	1
20 cm round cake	1
15 cm round cake	1
Hot apricot glaze	60 g
Yellow fondant	1.5 kg, rolled out into a thin sheet
White fondant	350 g
White royal icing	150 g

Equipment

30 cm round cake board	1
25 cm round cake board	1
20 cm round cake board	1
4 cm wide cotton lace	20 cm
Heart-shaped cookie cutter	1
2 cm wide gold ribbon	2 m
Piping bag	1
No. 2 writing tip	1
Long plastic dowels	7
Fresh roses	24
Baby's breath	2 stalks
Silver ribbons, fern and white netting	

Method

1 Glaze cakes with apricot glaze and cover with yellow fondant. Place cakes on cake boards. Set aside.

2 Roll out some white fondant to the length and width of lace, and about 0.25 cm thick. Place lace on fondant, press down and roll hard with a rolling pin to imprint lace pattern on fondant.

3 Trim fondant to the shape of lace with a sharp knife, then use a cookie cutter to trim opposite edge to shape of lace. Make enough fondant lace to go around 3 cakes.

4 Attach fondant lace around sides of each cake with some water. Trim off any overlap with a sharp knife. Fill a piping bag fitted with a writing tip with white royal icing and pipe a thin line of dots above lace to decorate.

5 Attach gold ribbon around base of each cake with a small amount of royal icing.

6 Insert 4 dowels each into largest and 3 into medium cake. Place medium cake on top of largest cake. Place smallest cake on top.

7 Make 8 small bouquets using roses, baby's breath, silver ribbons, ferns and netting. Position them between dowels and on top tier.

Congratulations

3

4

5

Cake and Decoration

15 cm round cake	1
Butter icing	100 g
Hot apricot glaze	40 g
Pale blue fondant	500 g, rolled out into a thin sheet
White royal icing	100 g
Silver dragees	

Equipment

Oval template (see pg 129)	1
20 cm square cake board	1
1 cm wide pale blue ribbon	30 cm, cut into 1.5 cm lengths
Ribbon inserter	1
Piping bag	1
No. 2 writing tip	1
Garrett frill cutter	1
Cocktail stick	1
Toy cradle	1
Small pale blue flowers	7–8

Method

1 Use template to cut cake into an oval shape. Slice cake horizontally to get 2 oval cake layers then sandwich with butter icing.

2 Brush cake with apricot glaze and cover with pale blue fondant. Place cake on cake board.

3 Cut 1 cm slots onto top of cake with small sharp knife. The distance between each slot should be about 2.5 cm.

4 Use a ribbon inserter to insert ribbons into slots.

5 Spoon some royal icing into a piping bag fitted with a writing tip and pipe small designs into spaces between each ribbon.

6 Roll out remaining pale blue fondant into a thin sheet and cut frills using a garrett frill cutter. Use a wooden cocktail stick to expand frills.

7 Moisten base of cake with some water and attach frills. Pipe a thin line of dots with royal icing just above frills. Attach dragees at intervals on dots.

8 Place small cradle with baby on top of cake and decorate with flowers.

Tip *Change the colour of the fondant, ribbons and flowers to pink if the baby is a girl.*

28

Love
Always

Here is my Heart

2

3

6

Cake and Decoration

18 cm heart-shaped cakes	2
Heart-shaped chocolates	12

Icing

Cream cheese	175 g
Creamy peanut butter	60 g
Vanilla essence	1 tsp
Icing (confectioner's) sugar	500 g, sifted
Strawberry emulco	1 Tbsp
Red food colouring	

Equipment

Overlapping heart template (see pg 130)	1
30 cm square cake board	1
Cake comb	1
Yellow sugarpaste flowers	1 bouquet

Method

1 Prepare icing. Beat cream cheese, peanut butter and vanilla essence together until smooth. Gradually add icing sugar and beat until fluffy. Mix in emulco and red colouring.

2 Using template, trim one cake.

3 Measure 1.5 cm from top of trimmed cake and use a serrated knife to slice a 1.5 cm layer off cake.

4 Slice other cake horizontally in half then sandwich together with icing.

5 Place both cakes on cake board. Secure cakes together with some icing. Spread remaining icing over top and sides of cakes.

6 Run a cake comb against side and over top of cakes to create a pattern all over.

7 Decorate cakes with chocolates and flowers.

32

Strawberry Surprise

4

5

8

Cake and Decoration

Fresh strawberries	500 g
Double or whipping cream	600 g
20 cm round cake	1

Equipment

25 cm round cake board	1
Piping bag	1
Ruby FM 820 or No. 44 star tip	1

Method

1. Hull half of strawberries and slice in quarters.

2. Whip double or whipping cream until stiff peaks form.

3. Slice cake horizontally to get 2 round cake layers. Place 1 layer on cake board and spread with 4 Tbsp double or whipped cream.

4. Arrange strawberry quarters on top of cream.

5. Sandwich with other cake layer and press down gently but firmly.

6. Cover top and side of cake with one-third of remaining cream. Spoon rest of cream into a piping bag fitted with a star tip.

7. Pipe rosettes around top and bottom edges and sides of cake.

8. Cut remaining strawberries into halves and use to decorate side of cake.

9. Pipe a large rosette on top of cake. Slice a large strawberry thinly and fan out. Press it into large rosette. Refrigerate cake if not serving immediately.

Queen of Hearts

Cake and Decoration

25 cm square cake	1
Egg whites	4
Salt	a pinch
Castor (superfine) sugar	100 g
Toasted almonds slices	80 g
Cherry pie filling	200 g

Equipment

8 cm heart-shaped pastry cutter	1
Piping bag	1
Bakery crafts no. 15 or No. 7 star tip	1

Method

1 Cut multiple heart-shaped cakes out of cake using a heart-shaped pastry cutter.

2 Whip egg whites until stiff then gradually beat in salt and sugar until a meringue is formed. Spread meringue on sides of cakes and cover with toasted almond slices.

3 Spoon cherry pie filling on top of cakes, leaving a 1 cm border from edge.

4 Place remaining meringue into a piping bag fitted with a star tip and pipe 2 rows of meringue stars around the pie filling.

5 Bake in a preheated oven at 210°C for 4–5 minutes or until tips of meringue turn brown. Serve immediately.

3

4

5

Cake and Decoration

20 cm round chocolate cake	1
White chocolate	100 g, grated
Heart-shaped chocolates	2
Hundreds-and-thousands (optional)	80 g

Truffle
Cooking chocolate	120 g
Icing (confectioner's) sugar	300 g
Butter	100 g
Double or whipping cream	60 ml

Glaze
Cooking chocolate	225 g
Double or whipping cream	115 ml

Equipment

Cake comb	1
20 cm round cake board	1
Piping bag	1
Ruby FM 809 or No. 8 star tip	1

Method

1 Prepare truffle. Melt cooking chocolate in a heatproof (flameproof) bowl placed over a pan of simmering water. Cool slightly. With a spoon, stir in icing sugar, butter and double or whipping cream until mixture is smooth and well blended. Set aside.

2 Prepare glaze. Heat cooking chocolate and double cream in a heavy-based saucepan over low heat, stirring until glaze is melted and smooth. Set aside to cool until it has a spreadable consistency.

3 Slice cake horizontally into 3. Place 1 layer on a wire rack lined with greaseproof paper underneath. Spread one-sixth of truffle mixture over.

4 Top with second cake layer, pressing down gently. Spread with another one-sixth of truffle mixture then top with third cake layer.

5 Pour glaze over cake and spread to cover cake completely. Using a cake comb, run along side and top of cake to create a pattern.

6 Carefully transfer cake to cake board. Spoon remaining truffle into a piping bag fitted with a star tip. Pipe a border at base of cake.

7 Pipe some truffle on top of cake then sprinkle grated white chocolate over. Place heart-shaped chocolates on cake and decorate cake board with hundreds-and-thousands as preferred.

Roses in the Box

2

4

6

Cake and Decoration

White fondant	300 g, rolled out into a thin sheet
Red royal icing	200 g
Pale pink fondant	600 g, rolled out into a thin sheet
15 cm square cake	1
Butter icing	250 g

Equipment

25 cm square cake board	1
1 cm wide red ribbon	1.2 m
15 cm square cake board	1
2 cm star cookie cutter	1
Piping bag	1
Bakery crafts no. 98 or No. 7 shell tip	1
1 cm wide silver ribbons, tied into bows	6
Fresh pink and red roses	12

Method

1 Moisten top of 25 cm cake board. Cover with white fondant then trim and neaten edges. Attach red ribbon around sides of cake board with some royal icing.

2 Moisten top and sides of 15 cm cake board. Cover with pale pink fondant. Reserve excess pale pink fondant. Press star cookie cutter into pale pink fondant to create a pattern. Set aside.

3 Slice cake horizontally to get 2 square layers then sandwich with some butter icing. Spread top and sides with remaining butter icing. Roll remaining pale pink fondant out and cover cake. Create a pattern all over cake with star cookie cutter.

4 Place cake onto the 25 cm cake board. Using a piping bag fitted with a shell tip, pipe shells of royal icing around base of cake.

5 Arrange silver ribbons, pink and red roses all over top, making sure front is higher than back.

6 Brush along back edge of cake with some water. Carefully place pale pink fondant-covered cake board on top as a cover, tilting it slightly. Attach cover to cake with a narrow strip of pale pink fondant.

Box of Chocolates

2

6

7

Cake and Decoration

18 cm heart-shaped cake	1
Butter icing	200 g
Royal icing	150 g
Pale blue fondant	500 g, rolled out into a thin sheet
White fondant	200 g, rolled out into a thin sheet
Foiled covered chocolates	18–20
Chocolate balls	20–25

Equipment

20 cm heart-shaped cake board	1
15 cm heart template (see pg 131)	1
Piping bag	1
No. 2 writing tip	1
18 cm heart template (see pg 131)	1
Garrett frill cutter	1
Cocktail stick	1

Method

1 Slice cake horizontally to get 2 heart-shaped layers then sandwich with butter icing. Place cake on cake board.

2 Use 15 cm heart-shaped template to cut a shallow heart from top of cake, leaving a 3 cm border around edge.

3 Cover cake with a thin layer of royal icing. Place remaining icing in a piping bag fitted with a writing tip. Set aside.

4 Measure height of cake. Cut a strip of pale blue fondant 2 cm wider than height of cake. Cover sides of cake with the strip, carefully smoothing it out all around top edge.

5 Use 18 cm heart-shaped template to cut a heart from white fondant sheet. Lay it in hollowed-out cake and trim off any excess.

6 Roll out excess pale blue fondant into a 0.3 cm thick sheet. Cut circles out with a garrett frill cutter. Halve circles. Roll a cocktail stick along fluted edge of each semi-circle to stretch it. Continue doing this until there are enough frills to go around cake.

7 Attach frills to cake with a little water. Pipe royal icing around cake to complete decoration.

8 Arrange chocolates attractively in heart-shaped box.

Iced Rosies

1

3

4

Cake and Decoration

Dark red rose petals	8–10 per small cake
Pink rose petals	8–10 per small cake
Egg white	1, lightly beaten
Castor (superfine) sugar	50 g
25 cm square cake	1
Butter icing	120 g
Red food colouring	

Orange Icing

Icing (confectioner's) sugar	150 g
Orange juice	1–2 Tbsp
Hot water	2–3 Tbsp

Equipment

8 cm round pastry cutter	1
Piping bag	1
No. 2 writing tip	1
10 cm round doilies	9

Method

1 Brush rose petals with beaten egg white and coat with sugar. Set aside for 2 hours.

2 Use round pastry cutter to cut 9 rounds out of cake. Cut cakes horizontally and sandwich with butter icing. Place cakes on a wire rack lined with greaseproof paper underneath.

3 Prepare orange icing. Mix icing sugar, orange juice and hot water. Spoon over cakes and allow icing to run down sides.

4 Colour remaining icing with a drop of red colouring to yield a delicate pink colour. Spoon into a piping bag fitted with a writing tip. Pipe lines on top of cakes.

5 Carefully transfer cakes onto doilies then spread a thin layer of orange icing around side of cakes.

6 Decorate sides with frosted rose petals.

Christmas Joy

Basket of Poinsettias

Cake and Decoration

15 cm round cake	1
Butter icing	200 g
Chocolate butter icing	250 g
Green sugar	60 g

Equipment

Aluminium foil	1 sheet, 30 x 20 cm
2 cm wide gold ribbon	60 cm
Cellophane tape	
15 cm round cake board	1
Piping bag	1
Ruby FM 803 ribbon tip	1
Poinsettias	4 flowers and leaves

Method

1. Fold aluminium foil lengthwise into a 2 cm wide strip. Wind gold ribbon around and secure with cellophane tape. Set aside for handle of basket.

2. Slice cake horizontally to get 2 round cake layers then sandwich with butter icing. Place cake on cake board.

3. Spread top and sides of cake with a thin layer of butter icing.

4. Spoon chocolate butter icing into a piping bag fitted with a shell tip. Pipe basket weave patterns around side of cake.

5. Arrange poinsettias on top of cake.

6. Press ends of handle into cake.

7. Carefully transfer basket of poinsettias onto a serving plate. Cover with green sugar.

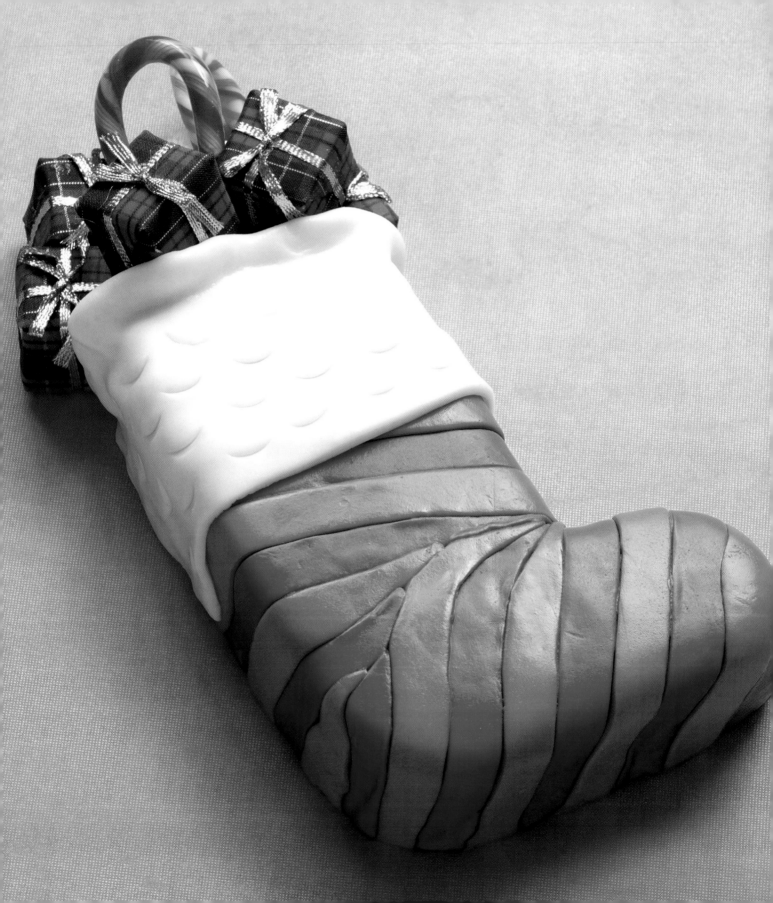

Stocking of Gifts

Cake and Decoration

15 cm square cake	1
Hot apricot glaze	40 g
Green fondant	250 g, rolled into a thin sheet
Red fondant	250 g, rolled into a thin sheet
White fondant	800 g
Candy canes	2

Equipment

30 cm square cake board	1
Wrapped gift boxes	5–6
Piping tip	1

Method

1 Cut cake vertically in half to get 2 rectangular cakes, one measuring 15 x 9 cm and the other 15 x 6 cm. Place narrower cake at base of wider one to form an L-shaped stocking.

2 Trim around edges of toe and heel to make them rounded. Assemble cake on cake board. Brush sides of cake that meet with apricot glaze and join.

3 Cut green fondant sheet into 12 strips, each 20 x 2 cm. Repeat with red fondant sheet.

4 Brush top and sides of cake with apricot glaze. Roll 600 g white fondant into a thin sheet and cover cake.

5 Stick alternating green and red strips diagonally on stocking with a little water. Trim to fit neatly. Arrange wrapped gifts and candy cane at top of stocking.

6 Roll remaining white fondant into a thick sheet measuring 25 x 13 cm for cuff of stocking. Moisten top of stocking with water and lay cuff into position so that it overlaps gifts slightly.

7 Create patterns on white fondant using a piping tip.

Gifts

Cake and Decoration

20 cm square cake	1
Hot apricot glaze	60 g
Pale yellow fondant	350 g, rolled out into a thin sheet
Orange royal icing	80 g
White royal icing	250 g
Purple fondant	450 g, rolled out into a thin sheet
Pink fondant	450 g, rolled out into a thin sheet
Silver dragees	
White fondant	620 g
Green fondant	250 g
Orange-red fondant	300 g

Equipment

Piping bags	2
No. 2 writing tip	1
5 cm wide taffeta ribbon	50 cm
Leaf-shaped cutter	1
1 cm wide silver ribbon	50 cm
25 cm square cake board	1

Method

1. Cut cake into a 12 cm square, an 8 cm square and two 12 x 8 cm cakes. Cut 12 cm square diagonally into 2 triangles.

2. Brush 8 cm square cake with apricot glaze and cover with pale yellow fondant. Using a piping bag fitted with a writing tip, pipe orange royal icing across to decorate. Set aside.

3. Brush a 12 x 8 cm cake with apricot glaze and cover with purple fondant. Using a piping bag fitted with a writing tip, pipe filigree of white royal icing on top. Set aside.

4. Brush remaining 12 x 8 cm cake with apricot glaze and cover with pink fondant. Pipe small dots of white royal icing and attach silver dragees. Tie 5 cm wide ribbon around cake. Set aside.

5. Partially knead 200 g white fondant together with 70 g green fondant to create a marbled effect. Brush a triangular cake with apricot glaze and cover with marbled fondant. Roll out remaining green fondant and cut out enough leaves with cutter. Attach leaves to cake with a little water.

6. Glaze remaining cake. Roll out orange-red fondant and cover cake. Tie a silver ribbon around it and attach a small bow on top with some royal icing. Arrange cakes attractively on cake board.

Fancy Candles

1

2

6

Cake and Decoration

Orange-red fondant	80 g
14 x 8 cm Swiss roll	1
Chocolate butter icing	300 g
Chocolate rice	80 g
8 x 6 cm Swiss roll	1
12 x 6 cm Swiss roll	1
10 x 10 cm Swiss roll	1
Butter icing	250 g
Green desiccated coconut	40 g
Chocolate buttons	50–60 g
White fondant	120 g, rolled out into a thin sheet
Yellow sugar	80 g

Equipment

Cocktail sticks	4, painted black
20 cm square cake board	1

Method

1 Shape orange-red fondant into 4 flames and insert a cocktail stick into the base of each flame. Leave to dry for 2 hours.

2 Cover tallest cake with some chocolate butter icing and roll in chocolate rice. Place upright on cake board.

3 Spread shortest cake with remaining chocolate butter icing and run a fork from the base upwards to make vertical lines. (Alternatively, place icing into a piping bag fitted with a ribbon tip and pipe vertical lines around cake.) Position it upright next to tallest cake on cake board.

4 Cover remaining 2 cakes with butter icing. Coat shorter cake with desiccated coconut. Assemble it upright on cake board.

5 Stick chocolate buttons onto last cake and position it with other cakes on cake board.

6 Cut out 4 circles, large enough to cover top of each cake, from white fondant sheet. Attach into position and stick a flame on top of each cake.

7 Sprinkle yellow sugar on cake board.

Snowman

Cake and Decoration

10 cm bowl-shaped cake	1
15 cm round cake	1
15 cm bowl-shaped cake	1
Brown chocolate buttons	2
Red chocolate buttons	3
Chocolate-coated pretzel sticks	2
Green sour jelly strips	2–3
Icing (confectioner's) sugar for dusting	

Icing

Castor (superfine) sugar	175 g
Egg white	1
Hot water	2 Tbsp
Salt	1 pinch

Equipment

25 cm round cake board	1
Bamboo skewers	4
Snowman's hat (see pg 132–3)	1

Method

1   Combine icing ingredients in a bowl and place over a pan of hot water. Whisk for about 5–7 minutes or until thick. Set aside.

2   Trim 10 cm bowl-shaped cake into a ball shape.

3   Place round cake on cake board, spread some icing on it and position larger bowl-shaped cake on top. Trim to create shape of body.

4   Insert 4 skewers into larger cake then place ball-shaped cake on top for head of snowman. Skewers will secure it in position.

5   Cover both cakes with icing. Attach brown chocolate buttons for eyes and red ones for buttons. Use chocolate pretzels for arms and nose, and jelly strips for scarf. Place black hat on top of snowman's head.

6   Spread remaining icing on exposed cake board then sift icing sugar all over for a snowy effect.

Fir Tree

1

3

5

Cake and Decoration

20 cm square cake	1
Vanilla butter icing	160 g
Green butter icing	250 g
Cocoa butter icing	100 g
Green desiccated coconut	80 g
Silver dragees	30 g

Equipment

Fir tree template (see pg 134)	1
25 cm square cake board	1
Piping bag	1
Ruby FM 820 star tip	1
Christmas ornaments	

Method

1. Place fir tree template on cake and trim cake to get basic shape of tree.
2. Slice cake horizontally to get 2 cake layers then sandwich with some vanilla butter icing.
3. Place cake on cake board. Spread green butter icing onto tree for leaves. Do not spread onto trunk of tree.
4. Spread cocoa butter icing onto trunk of tree.
5. Sprinkle green desiccated coconut onto green butter icing.
6. Place remaining vanilla butter icing into a piping bag fitted with a star tip. Pipe 2 lines on tree as streamers.
7. Decorate tree with dragees and Christmas ornaments.

Christmas on a Hill

1

3

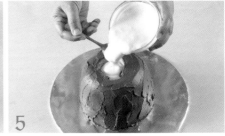
5

Cake and Decoration

20 cm bowl-shaped cake	1
Butter icing	120 g
Green desiccated coconut	80 g
Icing (confectioner's) sugar for dusting	

Cocoa Icing

Cocoa powder	2 Tbsp
Hot water	45 ml
Butter	75 g
Icing (confectioner's) sugar	250 g, sifted

Vanilla Icing

Icing (confectioner's) sugar	90 g, sifted
Hot milk	1–2 Tbsp
Vanilla essence	¹/₂ tsp

Equipment

25 cm round cake board	1
Fir trees, reindeers and cottage ornaments	

Method

1 Scoop out a small portion from top of cake and reserve for eating or discard. Slice cake horizontally then sandwich with butter icing.

2 Trim side of cake a little to create a small plateau to place cottage. Place cake on cake board.

3 Prepare cocoa icing. Dissolve cocoa powder in hot water and set aside to cool. Beat butter with half the icing sugar until light and fluffy. Add cooled cocoa mixture and remaining icing sugar. Beat well and spread over cake.

4 Moisten exposed cake board and spoon desiccated coconut over to cover. Arrange fir trees and reindeers on or around hill. Place cottage on plateau.

5 Prepare vanilla icing. Combine icing sugar, hot milk and vanilla essence. Stir until a smooth consistency is reached. Slowly pour into hollowed out cake top and let some drip down sides of cake.

6 Sift icing sugar on top for a snowy effect.

Specially
for the
Children

Space Rocket

Cake and Decoration

Butter icing	300 g
Cocoa powder	1 Tbsp
Demerara sugar	2 Tbsp
16 x 8 cm Swiss roll	1
Purple butter icing	250 g
Chocolate wafer bars	4
Chocolate buttons	20–25

Equipment

25 cm square cake board	1
Piping bag	1
Silver-coloured paper	1, cut into a 15 cm circle
Toy astronauts and space ornaments	

Method

1 Spread cake board with butter icing and rough it up to look like a moonscape. Dust with cocoa powder and sprinkle demerara sugar over.

2 Trim ends of Swiss roll and place it upright in the middle of cake board.

3 Cover Swiss roll with purple butter icing. Spoon remaining purple butter icing into a piping bag. Set aside.

4 Place chocolate wafer bars against rocket as support.

5 Make a cut through silver paper circle, stopping at the centre. Fold it into a cone to fit onto top of rocket. Position in place.

6 Snip end of piping bag and pipe small dots of purple icing onto rocket. Stick some chocolate buttons around to decorate.

7 Place toys and ornaments on cake board.

Train of Goodies

1

4

6

Cake and Decoration

22 cm loaf cakes	2
Butter icing	350 g
Yellow fondant	250 g, rolled out into a thin sheet
Chocolate butter icing	120 g
Light brown fondant	250 g, rolled out into a thin sheet
Green desiccated coconut	150 g
Sweets, chocolates and jelly sweets	

Equipment

Piping bag	1
No. 2 writing tip	1
30 cm square cake board	1
Toy trees	

Method

1 Cut each cake vertically into half to get 4 cakes. Shape one cake into the head of a train.

2 Score a 0.5 cm border around top edge of other 3 cakes and scrape out insides to make a shallow hollow for train's carriages.

3 Spread butter icing over train's head and carriages. Trim yellow fondant and stick onto windscreen and side windows of train's head.

4 Spoon chocolate butter icing into a piping bag fitted with writing tip. Pipe frames of windscreen and side windows onto train's head.

5 Trim light brown fondant sheet into a square to cover hollowed out carriages. Position in place.

6 Moisten cake board with water and sprinkle with desiccated coconut, leaving an area uncovered as train's track. Use chocolate butter icing to pipe train's tracks.

7 Attach some sweets as train's wheels and headlights. Place remaining sweets, chocolates and jelly sweets as cargo in train's carriages. Assemble cake on cake board.

Cars on the Road

1

3

5

Cake and Decoration

Grey fondant	250 g, rolled out into a thin sheet
Red, yellow and green chocolate buttons	1 each
Green royal icing	350 g
White fondant	80 g, rolled out into a thin strip
20 cm square cake	1
Butter icing	150 g

Equipment

25 cm square cake board	1
Cocktail stick	1, painted black
Toy cars, man and shrubs	

Method

1. Shape some grey fondant into a 2.5 x 1 cm traffic light stand and insert a cocktail stick along its length to strengthen it. Attach chocolate buttons on traffic light with some green royal icing. Allow to set for 1 hour.

2. Cut out thin strips of white fondant, each measuring 4 x 0.5 cm to represent white dividing lines on the road.

3. Roll remaining grey fondant out and cut into a 6 cm wide, L-shaped strip.

4. Cut cake horizontally to get 2 square cake layers then sandwich with some butter icing. Place cake on cake board.

5. Spread green royal icing on top and sides of cake then position grey fondant strip on cake. Stick white fondant strips onto middle of grey fondant strip.

6. Position toy cars, man, shrubs and traffic light in place.

Fish in a Dish

1

3

4

Cake and Decoration

20 cm round cake	1
Blue fondant	180 g, rolled out into a thin sheet
Butter icing	450 g
Orange fondant	450 g, rolled out into a thin sheet
Orange food colouring	
Red glacé cherry	1
Grey fondant	150 g
White royal icing	80 g

Equipment

Fish template (see pg 135)	1
25 cm round cake board	1
Piping bag	1
No. 5 petal tip	1

Method

1. Place fish template on cake and cut out fish shape. Trim to smoothen sides and ensure outside edges of fish slopes downwards.

2. Moisten cake board and cover with blue fondant. Place cake on cake board.

3. Spread a thin layer of butter icing over cake and cover with orange fondant.

4. Add orange colouring to remaining butter icing and spoon it into a piping bag fitted with a petal tip. Pipe scales on fish's body, avoiding gill section. Attach cherry for fish's eye.

5. Cover tail with grey fondant and make lines with the spine of a knife.

6. Spread white royal icing around cake board with a palette knife, roughing it up as waves.

Colourful Butterfly

2

3

7

Cake and Decoration

20 cm round cake	1
Cocoa butter icing	350 g
20 x 7 cm Swiss roll	1
Chocolate sprinkles	60–70 g
Hundreds and thousands	50–60 g
Roasted sunflower seeds	60–70 g
Strawberry chocolate chips	60–70 g
Chocolate butter icing	80 g
Red glacé cherry	1, halved
Green sugar	100 g

Equipment

25 cm square cake board	1
Butterfly's wings template (see pg 136)	1
Piping bag	1
20 cm green florist wires	2

Method

1   Slice cake horizontally to get 2 round cake layers then sandwich with some cocoa butter icing.

2   Cut cake into 2 semi-circles then use butterfly's wings template to shape butterfly's wings. Place wings onto cake board about 7 cm apart.

3   Place Swiss roll on centre of cake board for butterfly's body and arrange wings beside it. Trim body to fit.

4   Stick butterfly's wings on both sides of body with cocoa butter icing.

5   Spread cocoa butter icing all over cake. Stick desired decoration (chocolate sprinkles, hundreds and thousands, sunflower seeds and strawberry chocolate chips) as patterns on butterfly's wings.

6   Fill a piping bag with chocolate butter icing and snip tip. Pipe lines across butterfly's body. Arrange cherry halves in position for eyes.

7   Shape wire and stick on top of head for feelers.

8   Moisten exposed cake board and spoon green sugar over to cover.

Pink Princess

Cake and Decoration

20 cm round cake	1
Royal icing	250 g
15 cm bowl-shaped cake	1
Dark pink fondant	150 g, rolled out into a thin sheet
Pink fondant	450 g, rolled out into a thin sheet
Pink dragees	

Equipment

20 cm round cake board	1
13 cm body of doll (waist upwards)	1
Garrett frill cutter	1
Cocktail stick	1
Piping bag	1
Bakery crafts no. 98 shell tip	1
Small posy	1

Method

1 Place round cake on cake board. Spread with some royal icing and place bowl-shaped cake on top. Trim to create doll's skirt. Insert doll into cake.

2 Measure length of skirt from waist of doll to base of cake. Add 2 cm to this measurement and use it to measure and cut an isosceles triangle of dark pink fondant with a base of 6 cm for the skirt ((length + 2 cm) x 6 cm). Trim off top tip of triangle at the 2 cm mark. Set aside.

3 Spread royal icing on cake and attach dark pink fondant skirt over the front portion.

4 Use a garrett frill cutter to cut out a circle from dark pink fondant and halve it. Roll a cocktail stick along fluted edge of semi-circles to create frills. Attach to bottom of dark pink skirt with some water.

5 Measure and cut out pink fondant sheet to fit remaining part of skirt. Repeat previous step to get enough pink frills to go around pink skirt. Attach to pink skirt. Reserve excess pink fondant.

6 Fill a piping bag fitted with a star tip with royal icing and pipe shells along straight edge of frill and dots on pink skirt. Attach dragees on dots.

7 Roll out remaining pink fondant for doll's blouse. Decorate as desired then assemble posy for hair.

2

4

5

Cake and Decoration

15 cm round cake	1
Butter icing	250 g
White fondant	800 g
Blue fondant	350 g, rolled out into a thin sheet
Rainbow sprinkles	

Equipment

25 cm round cake board	1
Toy tea set	
Assorted toy vegetables	

Method

1. Slice cake horizontally to get 2 round cake layers and sandwich with some butter icing. Place cake on cake board. Spread top and sides of cake with remaining butter icing.

2. Roll out 450 g of white fondant into a 25 cm circle. Lay it on top of cake and allow it to fall into folds down the sides.

3. Roll out remaining white fondant. Cut out enough squares, each measuring 3 x 3 cm for tablecloth. Repeat for blue fondant.

4. Starting with a blue square in the centre of the cake, build up a chequered pattern, securing squares with water.

5. When squares are in place, run over surface of cake with a cake smoother to ensure squares lie neat and flat.

6. Arrange tea set on cake. Fill with rainbow sprinkles and assorted vegetables.

Hedgehog

3

5

6

Cake and Decoration

20 cm round cake	1
Roasted almonds shreds	80 g
Red glacé cherries	2
Dark brown chocolate button	1
Brown desiccated coconut	80 g

Chocolate Icing

Egg whites	2 (from 2 large eggs)
Icing (confectioner's) sugar	125 g
Unsalted butter	125 g
Cooking chocolate	50 g, melted and cooled

Equipment

25 cm square cake board	1

Method

1 Prepare chocolate icing. With an electric hand mixer, whisk egg whites and icing sugar over a pan of simmering water until mixture is firm and holds its shape. Remove from heat and cool slightly.

2 Beat butter until soft, then add cooled mixture a little at a time. Finally, add melted chocolate and stir well.

3 Slice cake vertically to get 2 semi-circles. Stand cakes on cut surface and sandwich together with some icing.

4 Trim one end of cake to form nose of hedgehog. Carefully place cake on cake board.

5 Smooth chocolate icing over cake. Use a fork to draw lines all over.

6 Stick in almond shreds for spikes. Position glacé cherries for eyes and chocolate button for nose.

7 Moisten exposed cake board and spoon brown desiccated coconut over.

Erupting Volcano

3

4

6

Cake and Decoration

20 cm round cake	1
Cocoa butter icing	300 g
15 cm bowl-shaped cake	1
Grey fondant	70 g
Chocolate-coated pretzel sticks	5–6, each broken into 3 pieces
Brown desiccated coconut	50 g
Green desiccated coconut	50 g

Glaze Icing

Icing sugar	80 g
Hot water	1 Tbsp
Red food colouring	

Equipment

20 cm square cake board	1
Toy trees	

Method

1. Place round cake on cake board. Spread some cocoa butter icing on top and position bowl-shaped cake centrally on it. Trim both cakes to resemble a volcano.

2. Scoop out a portion from top of cake to create a small crater.

3. Spread remaining cocoa butter icing over cake and exposed cake board.

4. Shape grey fondant into solidifying lava. Place randomly on cake.

5. Assemble chocolate-coated pretzel sticks as burnt forest. Sprinkle brown desiccated coconut over. Arrange toy trees on other side of volcano.

6. Prepare glaze icing. Mix icing sugar and hot water until smooth. Add red colouring. Slowly pour red glaze icing into crater and allow some to flow down.

2   3   4

Cake and Decoration

20 cm square cake	1
Chocolate butter icing	300 g
Blue piping jelly	80 g
Green desiccated coconut	50 g

Equipment

25 cm square cake board	1
Tear drop-shaped pond template (see pg 136)	1
Piping bag	1
Sugarpaste flowers	
Toy animals, trees and fence	

Method

1   Slice cake horizontally to get 2 square layers then sandwich with chocolate butter icing.

2   Place cake on cake board and use template to cut out pond. Use cut-out cake to create a small hill. Attach with some butter icing.

3   Spread chocolate butter icing all over cake, avoiding pond area but making sure pond boundary is slightly higher than surrounding area.

4   Spoon blue piping jelly into a piping bag and snip off tip. Pipe jelly into pond area. Sprinkle green desiccated coconut on chocolate butter icing to create grass around pond.

5   Arrange sugarpaste flowers around pond. Position toy animals, trees and fence on top.

Dip in the Pool

2

3

4

Cake and Decoration

20 cm square cake	1
Butter icing	350 g
White fondant	800 g, rolled out into a thin sheet
Black royal icing	50 g
Blue royal icing	250 g

Equipment

30 cm square cake board	1
Piping bag	1
No. 2 writing tip	1
Small toy swimmers and pool ornaments	
2 cm wide pale blue ribbon	1 m

Method

1 Slice cake horizontally to get 2 square cake layers then sandwich with some butter icing.

2 Cut a portion of cake measuring 20 x 5 cm off one side of cake then place it against the width of larger cake to increase its length. Trim to fit. Place on cake board. Attach both pieces with some butter icing.

3 Spread remaining butter icing over top and sides of cake then cover cake with white fondant. Roll out excess white fondant into a 1 cm thick sheet and cut out 4 strips, 2 measuring 18 x 2 cm, 1 measuring 15 x 5 cm and another measuring 15 x 2 cm. Attach strips around sides of pool with a little water.

4 Place black royal icing into a piping bag fitted with a writing tip and pipe criss-cross lines as tiles on side of pool.

5 Spread blue royal icing inside pool. Assemble figurines in pool or on pool's side.

6 Attach pale blue ribbon around base with some royal icing.

Boat on a Lake

Cake and Decoration

20 cm round cake	1
Butter icing	350 g
Green butter icing	120 g
Demerara sugar	120 g
Cocoa butter icing	40 g
Purple butter icing	80 g
Chocolate rocks	40–50 g
Toasted almond slices	60 g
Blue piping jelly	120–130 g

Equipment

25 cm round cake board	1
Piping bags	4
Bakery crafts no. 66 or No. 5 leaf tip	1
Ruby FM 809 star tip	1
Toy boat and swimmer	

Method

1 Slice cake horizontally into 2 round layers then sandwich with some butter icing. Place cake on cake board. Spread some butter icing over top and sides of cake.

2 Spoon remaining butter icing into a piping bag and snip 0.4 cm off the tip. Pipe an outline of a pond on top of cake.

3 Spoon green butter icing into a piping bag fitted with a leaf tip. Pipe long-bladed leaves around pond and side of cake.

4 Moisten exposed cake board with water and cover with demerara sugar.

5 Spoon cocoa butter icing into a piping bag fitted with a star tip. Pipe a short line halfway along the border of pond.

6 Spoon purple butter icing into a piping bag and snip 0.3 cm off the tip. Pipe flowers randomly onto leaves and pond area.

7 Arrange chocolate rocks as a path and almond slices as ground.

8 Spread blue piping jelly into pond area. Place boat and swimmer on pond.

Loving Football

2   3   5

Cake and Decoration

25 cm square cake	1
Butter icing	120 g
Green butter icing	200 g
Green desiccated coconut	140 g
Green food colouring	

Glaze Icing

Icing (confectioner's) sugar	250 g
Hot water	2 Tbsp

Equipment

25 cm square cake board	1
Piping bags	2
Ruby FM 824 star tip	1
Toy football players	2
No. 2 writing tip	1

Method

1. Cut off 5 cm from one side of cake and discard. Slice cake horizontally to get 2 cake layers then sandwich with butter icing. Place on cake board.

2. Spread green butter icing around sides of cake. Press green desiccated coconut onto it.

3. Place remaining green butter icing in a piping bag fitted with a star tip and pipe a straight border around the top edge of cake.

4. Prepare glaze icing. Mix icing sugar and hot water until smooth. Spoon 2 Tbsp glaze icing into a piping bag fitted with a writing tip. Set aside.

5. Colour remaining glaze icing green and use to coat top of cake. Leave to set.

6. Pipe football field lines on cake with glaze icing. Place figurines and goal posts on field.

Tunnel and Train

Cake and Decoration

15 cm square cake	1
Cocoa butter icing	350 g
Chocolate sprinkles	120 g
Chocolate rocks	100 g

Equipment

25 cm square cake board	1
Toy railway conductor and tracks	
4 cm high toy train	1

Method

1 Cut cake vertically to get 2 rectangles. Stand cakes on cut surface. Sandwich together with some cocoa butter icing.

2 Carve top corners of cake to create outside of tunnel.

3 Cut out a 6 x 5 cm tunnel from one end of cake.

4 Place cake on cake board and cover with some cocoa butter icing. Coat top and sides with chocolate sprinkles.

5 Place tracks and railway conductor outside tunnel. Position toy train on tracks. Sprinkle chocolate rocks around train and tracks.

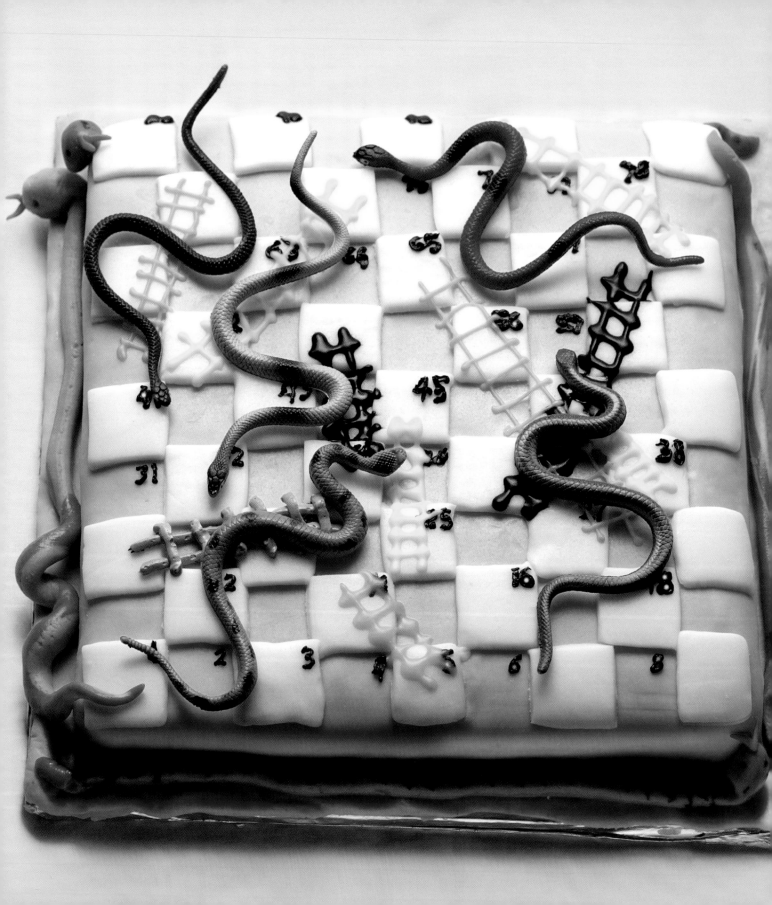

Snakes and Ladders

4

5

7

Cake and Decoration

20 cm square cake	1
Butter icing	300 g
Green fondant	750 g, rolled out into a thin sheet
White fondant	250 g, rolled out into a thin sheet
Brown fondant	150 g
Orange fondant	150 g
Pink fondant	150 g
Brown, black, red food colouring	
Black royal icing	60 g
Yellow royal icing	80 g
Purple royal icing	50 g
Orange royal icing	60 g

Equipment

25 cm square cake board	1
Cake smoother	1
Fine tip paintbrush	1
Piping bags	4
No. 2 writing tips	1
Toy snakes	7

Method

1 Slice cake horizontally to get 2 square cake layers then sandwich with some butter icing. Place cake on cake board and spread top and sides with remaining butter icing.

2 Cover cake and cake board with green fondant.

3 Cut 45 squares of white fondant measuring 2 cm each and stick onto cake in a chequered pattern. Press gently down with a cake smoother.

4 Shape brown fondant into 2 snakes, each 20 cm long. Repeat procedure with orange and pink fondant, or use a combination of the colours to make 2 more snakes.

5 Paint pattern on snakes using paintbrush and food colouring. Attach snakes to base of cake with a little water.

6 Place black royal icing into a piping bag fitted with a writing tip. Pipe numbers on cake.

7 Place yellow, purple and orange royal icing into separate piping bags. Snip tips off and pipe ladders on cake.

8 Allow icing to set then arrange toy snakes on cake.

Green Monster

3

4

5

Cake and Decoration

15 cm bowl-shaped cake	1
Butter icing	160 g
Green fondant	500 g, rolled out into a thin sheet
Black fondant	60 g
White fondant	40 g
Dark red sweets	2
Royal icing	2 Tbsp
Red food colouring	

Equipment

25 cm round cake board	1
Piping bag	1
Toy Halloween ornaments	

Method

1 Slice cake horizontally and sandwich with one-third of butter icing.

2 Place cake on cake board. Cover with remaining butter icing then green fondant sheet, carefully stretching fondant sheet to edge of cake board.

3 Shape black fondant for monster's eyebrows and mouth. Stick in place with a little water.

4 Shape white fondant for fangs. Position under upper lip. Attach red sweets for eyeballs.

5 Slacken royal icing with a few drops of water and colour it red. Put into a piping bag and snip the tip off. Pipe red icing around monster's mouth.

6 Decorate with Halloween ornaments.

Horror Sorcerer

3

4

5

Cake and Decoration

15 cm bowl-shaped cake	1
Black fondant	100 g
White fondant	50 g
Red fondant	40 g
Chocolate rocks	60–70 g

Coffee Icing

Instant coffee granules	1 tsp
Cocoa powder	2 Tbsp
Hot milk	60 ml
Butter	125 g
Icing (confectioner's) sugar	300 g

Equipment

20 cm round cake board	1
Toy Halloween ornaments and snake	

Method

1 Prepare coffee icing. Combine coffee granules, cocoa powder and hot milk. Leave to cool slightly. Beat butter with half the icing sugar until creamy. Add coffee mixture and remaining icing sugar then beat well.

2 Slice cake horizontally and sandwich with coffee icing. Place on cake board.

3 Hollow out a portion of cake near base to look like the entrance of a cave. Spread remaining coffee icing all over cake.

4 Roll out black fondant and cut into shape for entrance of cave and eyebrows. Press black fondant for entrance into place.

5 Shape white fondant into fangs and stick them to the top of cave opening with some water. Attach eyebrows in place.

6 Shape red fondant into eyes and stick into place below eyebrows.

7 Arrange chocolate rocks, Halloween ornaments and snake in cave cavity and around entrance.

Treasure Chest

2

3

4

Cake and Decoration

18 cm square cake	1
Chocolate coins	
Cocoa butter icing	250 g
Chocolate butter icing	150 g

Equipment

Gold-coloured paper	1 sheet, 18 x 10 cm
25 cm square cake board	1
Piping bag	1
Bakery crafts no. 98 or No. 7 shell tip	1
Sequins (to be removed before cutting cake)	
Gold and silver beaded necklaces	

Method

1 Cut a third off one side of cake, leaving an 18 x 12 cm rectangular cake.

2 Run a sharp knife around the edges of cake to make them rounded like a chest. Create lid by cutting horizontally two-thirds from base and ending 2 cm from 'back' of chest.

3 Make another cut 2.5 cm above the first cut and slant knife downwards as you cut so that it meets the first cut.

4 Slide a palette knife in to support lid of chest and remove cut portion of cake. Immediately slide gold-coloured paper in at the base of exposed portion. Arrange chocolate coins on paper to support lid.

5 Transfer cake onto cake board.

6 Spread cocoa butter icing over top and sides of cake.

7 Spoon chocolate butter icing into a piping bag fitted with a shell tip. Pipe a shell border around base, down each of the 4 corners and around tip edge of chest. Pipe 2 bands across lid of chest. Attach sequins onto intersections.

8 Attach more chocolate coins and necklaces at the front of chest to create the look of an overflowing treasure chest.

Special
Occasions

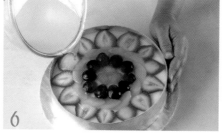

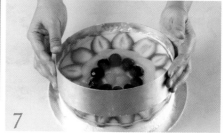

Cake and Decoration

20 cm vanilla sponge cake	1

Cream Cheese Layer

Water	3 Tbsp
Gelatine powder	1¹/₂ Tbsp
Cream cheese	500 g, at room temperature
Castor (superfine) sugar	100 g
Evaporated milk	100 ml, cold

Top Layer

Water	500 ml
Konnyaku jelly powder	1 Tbsp
Granulated sugar	40 g
Fresh or canned fruits	

Decoration

Butter icing	60 g
Croquants	50–60 g
Fresh or canned fruits	
Mint leaves	1 sprig

Equipment

22 cm round cake board	1
20 cm ring mould	1

Method

1 Prepare cream cheese layer. Put water in a small heatproof (flameproof) bowl, sprinkle gelatine powder over and set aside for 10 minutes. Place bowl over lightly simmering water then stir to dissolve gelatine. Allow to cool slightly.

2 In another bowl, beat cream cheese until smooth. Add sugar and beat until light and sugar has dissolved.

3 Pour in evaporated milk and beat well. Mix in gelatine mixture and beat to combine.

4 Place cake on cake board. Position ring mould in place around cake and pour cream cheese mixture in to cover. Allow to set in the refrigerator for 5 hours.

5 Prepare top layer. Bring water to the boil. Combine Konnyaku powder and sugar then gradually add into boiling water, 1 Tbsp at a time, stirring often until sugar dissolves. Remove from heat and set aside to cool slightly, stirring often to prevent it setting.

6 Arrange fresh or canned fruits on top of cream cheese layer. Carefully pour jelly mixture over. (Some fruits may not be submerged by the jelly.)

7 When set, gently loosen edge of cake with palette knife dipped in hot water, then remove ring mould.

8 Spread butter icing around sides of sponge cake and press croquants into it. Decorate cake with fresh or canned fruits and mint leaves.

Carrot Heart

2

5

6

Cake and Decoration

18 cm heart-shaped carrot cake	1
Croquants	80 g
Orange and green food colouring	
Marzipan	200 g

Icing

Cream cheese	250 g
Butter	90 g
Lemon juice	$^1/_2$ Tbsp
Icing (confectioner's) sugar	450 g

Equipment

20 cm heart-shaped cake board	1
Cake comb	1

Method

1 Prepare icing. Beat cream cheese, butter and lemon juice until smooth. Gradually add icing sugar, beating constantly until smooth.

2 Slice cake horizontally to get 2 heart-shaped cake layers then sandwich with some icing. Place cake on cake board. Spread top and sides of cake with remaining icing.

3 Use a palette knife to make an attractive swirling design all over cake.

4 Run a cake comb along the sides of cake to create ridges. Press croquants onto lower half.

5 Add orange colouring to 160 g marzipan and divide into 8 portions. Shape each portion into a carrot and mark segments on it with a knife.

6 Add green colouring to remaining marzipan and shape it into green leaves of carrots. Press the end of a brush into carrot top then insert green marzipan leaves. Decorate top of cake with completed carrots.

Springtime Flowers

Cake and Decoration

20 cm round cake	1
Butter icing	140 g
Almond halves	40, roasted
Red glacé cherries	8
Green sour jelly strips	6, cut to size
Demerara sugar	120 g

Orange Icing

Icing (confectioner's) sugar	160–175 g, sifted
Orange zest	from 1 orange
Orange juice	from 1 orange
Orange food colouring	

Equipment

25 cm round cake board	1

Method

1 Slice cake horizontally to get 2 round cake layers then sandwich with butter icing.

2 Place cake on a wire rack with a large piece of greaseproof paper underneath.

3 Prepare orange icing. Mix icing sugar, orange zest, juice and orange colouring. Beat well until smooth and spread over top and sides of cake.

4 Arrange 5 almond halves on cake to form petals of a flower. Create 8 flowers in total. Use glacé cherries as flower centres.

5 Position sour jelly strips to form flower stems.

6 Once icing has set, carefully transfer cake onto cake board.

7 Moisten exposed cake board and cover with demerara sugar.

Hat of Blossoms

Cake and Decoration

15 cm bowl-shaped cake	1
Royal icing	250 g
Pale yellow fondant	800 g, rolled out into a thin sheet
Marzipan	350 g

Equipment

30 cm round cake board	1
Piping bag	1
Bakery crafts no. 98 or No. 7 shell tip	1
Dark red sugarpaste flowers	1 bouquet

Method

1. Place cake on cake board. Spread royal icing to cover cake. Spoon remaining royal icing into a piping bag fitted with a shell tip. Set aside.

2. Cut pale yellow fondant into a 30 cm circle. Smooth fondant over cake and stretch to cover cake board.

3. Lift yellow fondant at intervals and support underside with marzipan to create rim of hat.

4. Pipe royal icing shells along outer edge of rim.

5. Arrange sugarpaste flowers to decorate.

Bowl of Eggs

1

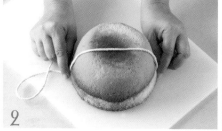

2

4

Cake and Decoration

15 cm round cake	1
15 cm bowl-shaped cake	1
Butter icing	250 g
Pale blue fondant	600 g, rolled out into a thin sheet
Yellow fondant	150 g
Red fondant	150 g
Green fondant	150 g
Assorted mini Easter eggs	20–25

Equipment

2.5 cm star cookie cutter	1
2.5 cm crescent cookie cutter	1
Pale yellow netting	50 cm
20 cm round cake board	1
Toy chicks	2

Method

1 Trim both cakes to flatten if necessary. Spread some butter icing onto round cake and place bowl cake on top. Hollow out a shallow circle from top of cake, leaving a 2 cm rim around edge.

2 Measure height of cake and its widest part. Cut pale blue fondant to this measurement, remembering to add width of rim to height.

3 Wrap pale blue fondant around cake, smoothing over gently to cover entire cake.

4 Cut out star and crescent shapes from yellow, red and green fondants. Secure onto sides of bowl with a little water.

5 Place yellow netting as covering over top of bowl. Assemble Easter eggs in bowl.

6 Place cake on cake board and position chicks on side of cake.

Happy Gardening

1

4

5

Cake and Decoration

18 cm hexagonal cake	1
Butter icing	350 g
Assorted nuts	150 g, chopped
Hot water	a few drops, if needed
Blue food colouring	

Lemon Icing

Icing (confectioner's) sugar	175 g
Lemon juice	from 1 lemon

Equipment

20 cm square cake board	1
Piping bags	2
No. 2 writing tip	1
Cocktail stick	1
Toy vegetables, gardening tools and farmer figurines	

Method

1 Slice cake horizontally to get 2 hexagonal cake layers then sandwich with some butter icing. Place cake on cake board. Cover sides with some butter icing and press nuts onto it.

2 Spoon remaining butter icing into a piping bag and snip off tip. Pipe zig-zag lines around edge of cake.

3 Prepare lemon icing. Mix icing sugar and lemon juice until smooth. If it is too thick, dilute with some hot water. Spoon 2 Tbsp into a small bowl and mix with a few drops of blue colouring. Spoon into a piping bag fitted with a writing tip.

4 Smooth remaining white icing on top of cake. Pipe circles of blue icing about 1 cm apart, starting at the centre and moving out towards the edge of cake.

5 Use a cocktail stick to cut across blue circles, alternating with side to centre and centre to side strokes. Allow to set.

6 Place vegetables, tools and farmers on top of cake.

Cake and Decoration

20 cm square cake	1
Hot apricot glaze	60 g
White fondant	800 g, rolled out into a thin sheet
Black food colouring	
Blue fondant	400 g
Pale yellow fondant	400 g
Marbled grey and white fondant	350 g
Black royal icing	40 g
Orange royal icing	40 g

Equipment

Fine tip paintbrush	1
14 cm square embroidered fabric	1 sheet
2 cm wide dark blue ribbon	3 cm
2 cm wide red ribbon	5 cm
1.5 cm wide black ribbon	4 cm
Piping bags	2
No. 2 writing tips	2
25 cm square cake board	1

Method

1 Cut cake into 3: (a) 12 x 10 cm, (b) 10 x 8 cm and (c) 16 x 10 cm. Set aside remaining portion of cake for eating or discard.

2 Brush cakes with hot apricot glaze and cover with a thin layer of white fondant. Use a sharp knife to make shallow indentations on 3 sides of each cake, creating pages of a book.

3 Paint textured sides with black food colouring. Set aside until paint is dry.

4 Roll blue fondant out into a 0.4 cm thick sheet. Create a textured surface on fondant by laying embroidered fabric on it and applying firm and even pressure with a rolling pin. Turn fondant over and brush with some water. Place cake (a) on blue fondant sheet and cut fondant to size, making it just slightly bigger than cake like a book's cover. Wrap fondant over cake and use the back of a knife to indent lines as spine of book. Make a slit at the base of cake and insert a dark blue ribbon as a book marker.

5 Repeat with pale yellow fondant and red ribbon for cake (b) and marbled grey and white fondant and black ribbon for cake (c). You may also choose not to emboss fondant.

6 Place black and orange royal icing into separate piping bags fitted with writing tips. Pipe letterings on books. Allow fondant to dry overnight before assembling books on cake board.

Pineapple Delight

Cake and Decoration

15 cm bowl-shaped cakes	2
Hot apricot glaze	40 g
Butter icing	200 g
Brownish-green fondant	150 g
Yellowish-green fondant	200 g, rolled out into a thin sheet
Light orange fondant	200 g
Bright orange fondant	250 g
Fresh fruits	

Equipment

20 cm round cake board	1
'V'-shaped cutter	1
Plastic pineapple leaves	

Method

1   Trim to flatten top of both cakes. Place one cake on its base on cake board and brush with hot apricot glaze. Place other cake on top to create rounded shape of pineapple.

2   Trim cakes to resemble shape of pineapple. Spread butter icing onto cakes.

3   Roll out coloured fondants and cut into long strips, each 3 cm wide. Using a 'V'-shaped cookie cutter, cut along one long edge of fondant to resemble pineapple segments.

4   Assemble strips onto cake, starting with the greener shades on top and the orange shades in the middle, then ending with the greener shades at the bottom again.

5   Position plastic pineapple leaves on top and decorate with fresh fruits.

119

Laces and Beads

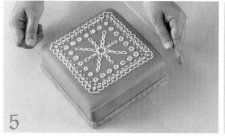

Cake and Decoration

White royal icing	150 g
15 cm square cake	1
Butter icing	250 g
Pink fondant	250 g, rolled out into a thin sheet
Silver dragees	

Equipment

Piping bag	1
No. 2 writing tip	1
20 cm square cake board	1
20 cm square glass sheet	1
Square doily template (see pg 137)	1
Spoon/fork with decorative handle	1
4 cm wide lace ribbon	70 cm
Silver beaded chain	1 m

Method

1. Spoon white royal icing into a piping bag fitted with a writing tip. Place a sheet of glass on doily template. Pipe the pattern carefully. Set aside to harden.

2. Slice cake horizontally to get 2 square cake layers then sandwich with butter icing. Place cake on a cake board. Spread top and sides of cake with remaining butter icing.

3. Cover cake with pink fondant. Trim edges to neaten.

4. Roll out excess pink fondant into a long rope and attach to base of cake. Make patterns with the decorative handle of a spoon/fork.

5. Press hardened royal icing pattern onto top of cake.

6. Trace pattern using remaining royal icing in piping bag. Attach dragees on dots.

7. Tie lace ribbon around cake. Secure ends with royal icing. Press silver beaded chain around base of cake.

Techniques and Templates

All templates here are drawn to scale, so you can trace them directly from these pages without having to enlarge or shrink them.

Transferring Letterings onto Cakes

You can pipe letterings directly onto cakes if you have steady hands and are confidant of getting the proportions correct. Alternatively, use these templates and follow the instructions below.

Equipment

Clear glass sheet	1, large enough for lettering/characters
Piping bag	1
No. 1 or 2 writing tip	1
Royal icing	as needed

Applies to:

Cherry Blossoms

New Year Cheer

Method

1. Trace lettering onto a piece of paper. Carefully outline lettering on the back of the paper with a pencil.

2. Place design under glass sheet with outline facing you. The lettering should be back-to-front.

3. Using a piping bag fitted with a writing tip, pipe royal icing directly onto glass. Set aside to dry.

4. When icing is dry and quite hard, press it against fresh fondant or gelatine icing on cake. Lift glass away and an impression will be left on cake.

5. Pipe using impressions as a guide and continue to follow instructions on individual recipe.

Chinese New Year Greetings

HAPPY
CHINESE
NEW YEAR

財源廣進

Crescent for Blue Mosque

Equipment

Tracing paper
Gold-coloured
  cardboard   1 sheet, 4 x 4 cm
Glue
Cocktail stick   1

Method

1 Trace outline of crescent onto tracing paper.

2 Place design onto cardboard and cut out 2 crescent shapes.

3 Spread glue on crescent shapes then sandwich a cocktail stick
   in between. Leave half the cocktail stick exposed so it can be
   inserted into cake.

4 Set aside to dry before using.

Kolam

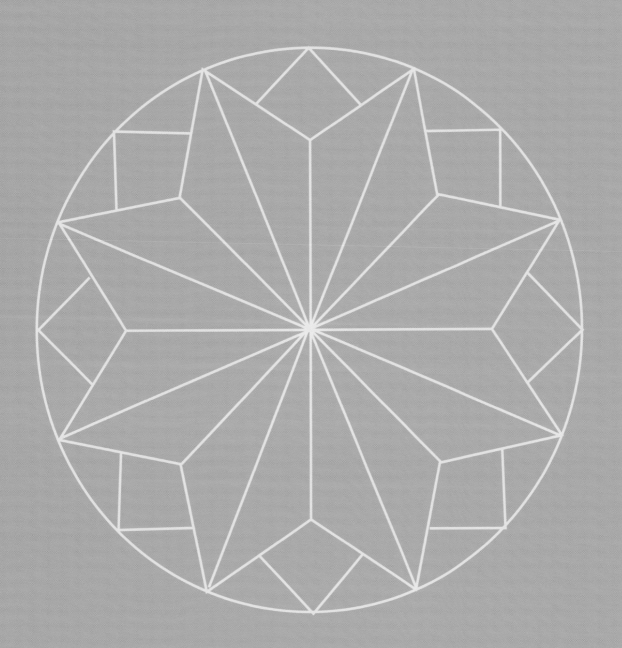

127

Assembling Mortarboards

Equipment

Tracing paper
Black cardboard   1 large sheet
Big needle   1
Ping pong balls   3, each cut in half
Glue
Cocktail sticks   2, cut into 6,
                         1 cm lengths
Thick red thread   1.8 m, cut into
                         10 cm lengths

Mortarboard
square top template

Method

1 Trace square design onto tracing paper.

2 Transfer design onto mounting board and cut out
   12 squares.

3 Using the needle, make a hole at the centre of each square
   and ping pong ball half.

4 Stick 2 squares together to create thicker boards.

5 Bunch 3 lengths of red thread together and fold into 2 to
   create a loop. Carefully insert the loop into the hole in a
   square board and then through a ping pong ball half. Use
   the big needle if necessary.

6 Insert a 1 cm cocktail stick into the loop inside the ping
   pong ball and pull threads so they fall nicely. Continue to
   make 5 more mortarboards.

Oval

Trace outline of oval onto
a sheet of paper and cut out template.
Use as a guide to trim cake.

Overlapping Heart

Trace outline of heart onto
a sheet of paper and cut out template.
Use as a guide to trim cake.

18 cm Heart

15 cm Heart

Trace outline of 15 cm or 18 cm heart
onto a sheet of paper and cut out template.
Use as a guide to trim cake.

Assembling Snowman's Hat

Equipment

Tracing paper
Black cardboard   1 A4-sized sheet
Glue

Method

1. Trace outline of both designs onto a piece of tracing paper.
2. Transfer design onto cardboard.
3. Cut out circle then cut and remove inner circle to create rim of hat. Set aside.
4. Cut out other design and make small snips around edge of rounded side, making sure cuts are 1 cm apart and do not exceed broken lines marked B.
5. Fold along broken lines, allowing cut sections to fan out.
6. Fold side A onto broken lines marked B to shape into a cone. Secure with glue.
7. Place cone onto a flat surface with cut sections fanned out. Put glue on the cut sections (facing upwards).
8. Carefully place rim of hat onto cut sections. Press firmly to stick.

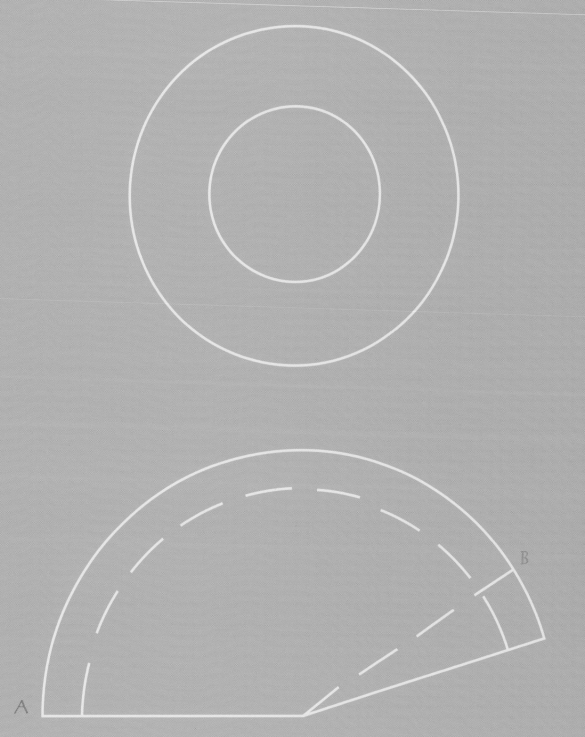

A

B

Fir Tree

Trace outline of fir tree onto
a sheet of paper and cut out template.
Use as a guide to trim cake.

Fish

Trace outline of fish onto a
sheet of paper and cut out template.
Use as a guide to trim cake.

Butterfly's Wings

Tear Drop-shaped Pond

Trace outline of butterfly's
wings onto a sheet of paper and
cut out template.
Use as a guide to trim cake.

Trace outline of pond onto
a sheet of paper and cut
out template. Use as
a guide to trim cake.

Square Doily

Basic Recipes

These basic recipes can be used with any of the cake recipes in this book unless otherwise specified in the individual recipes. Create something new every time by simply changing the flavour of the base cake!

140 Vanilla Madeira Cake

141 Orange Madeira Cake

142 Chocolate Madeira Cake

143 Marble Madeira Cake

144 Butter Cake

145 Coffee Cake

146 Swiss Roll

147 Carrot Cake

148 Strawberry Cake

149 Butter Icing (1) or Butter Cream

Butter Icing (2)

150 Chocolate Butter Icing

151 Cocoa Butter Icing

Vanilla Butter Icing

152 Royal Icing

Fondant or Sugarpaste (1)

153 Fondant or Sugarpaste (2)

154 Marzipan or Almond Paste

Coloured Desiccated Coconut or Sugar

155 Gelatine Icing

Blue Piping Jelly

Vanilla Madeira Cake

Ingredients

Butter for greasing	
Butter	115 g, softened
Castor (superfine) sugar	115 g
Eggs (Grade B)	2, lightly beaten
Self-raising flour	170 g
Fresh milk	1 Tbsp
Vanilla essence	1 tsp

Cake Tin Size

15 cm round cake tin

Method

1 Line a 15 cm round cake tin with greaseproof paper and grease well. Set aside.

2 Place softened butter and sugar in a large bowl. Add eggs.

3 Sift in flour and add milk and vanilla essence.

4 Using an electric mixer on a slow setting, bind all the ingredients together.

5 As soon as the ingredients are combined, increase speed and beat for 1 minute or until light. Level mixture into prepared tin and smooth top.

6 Bake in a preheated oven at 170°C for 1 hour or until a skewer inserted into the centre of cake comes out clean.

Orange Madeira Cake

Cake Tin Sizes

15 cm square cake tin

18 cm round cake tin

1 litre dome-shaped baking bowl

900 g loaf tin

Ingredients

Butter for greasing	
Plain (all-purpose) flour for dusting (optional)	
Butter	170 g, softened
Castor (superfine) sugar	170 g
Eggs (Grade B)	3
Self-raising flour	230 g
Orange rind	1 tsp
Freshly squeezed orange juice	2 Tbsp

Method

1　Line a cake tin with greaseproof paper and grease well. If using a bowl, omit greaseproof paper but grease well and dust with plain flour. Set aside.

2　Combine softened butter, sugar and eggs in a large bowl.

3　Sift in flour and add orange rind and juice.

4　Using an electric mixer on a slow setting, bind all the ingredients together.

5　As soon as the ingredients are well combined, increase speed and beat for 1 minute or until the mixture is light. Level into the prepared tin or bowl and smoothen the top.

6　Bake in a preheated oven at 170°C for 1 hour 25 minutes or until a skewer inserted into the centre of the cake comes out clean.

Chocolate Madeira Cake

Ingredients

Butter for greasing	
Butter	285 g, softened
Castor (superfine) sugar	285 g
Eggs (Grade B)	5
Self-raising flour	310 g
Cocoa powder	40 g
Fresh milk	3 Tbsp
Vanilla essence	1¹/₂ tsp

Cake Tin Size

18 cm square cake tin
20 cm round cake tin

Method

1 Line a cake tin with greaseproof paper and grease well. Set aside.

2 In a large bowl, combine softened butter, sugar and eggs.

3 Sift in flour and cocoa powder then add milk and vanilla essence.

4 Using an electric mixer at slow speed, beat for 30 seconds. Increase speed then beat for 1 minute more.

5 Spoon mixture into prepared tin and level the top.

6 Bake in a preheated oven at 170°C for 1 hour 30 minutes or until a skewer inserted into the centre of the cake comes out clean.

Marble Madeira cake

Cake Tin Sizes

20 cm square cake tin
23 cm round cake tin

Ingredients

Butter for greasing	
Butter	400 g, softened
Castor (superfine) sugar	400 g
Eggs (Grade B)	7
Self-raising flour	450 g
Fresh milk	60 ml
Chocolate emulco	$1\frac{1}{2}$ tsp
Coffee essence	1 tsp

Method

1 Line a cake tin with greaseproof paper and grease well.

2 In a large bowl, mix softened butter, sugar and eggs.

3 Sift in flour and add milk. Using an electric mixer at slow speed, beat until well combined. Increase to maximum speed and beat until light.

4 Divide cake mixture into two parts. Add chocolate emulco to one portion and coffee essence to the other.

5 Spoon both portions alternately into the prepared tin. Run the tip of a knife through the cake from the top to create a marbled effect.

6 Bake in a preheated oven at 170°C for 1 hour 45 minutes or until a skewer inserted into the centre of the cake comes out clean.

Butter Cake

Cake Tin Size

25 cm square cake tin

Ingredients

Butter for greasing	
Butter	450 g, softened
Castor (superfine) sugar	450 g
Eggs (Grade A)	6
Self-raising flour	550 g, sifted
Fresh milk	75 ml
Vanilla essence	2 tsp

Method

1 Line the cake tin with greaseproof paper then grease well. Set aside.

2 Using an electric mixer at high speed, beat softened butter and sugar until light and fluffy.

3 Add eggs one at a time, beating well after each addition.

4 Add flour alternately with milk. Mix well then add in vanilla essence.

5 Pour mixture into prepared tin and create a shallow well in the centre by pushing the batter towards the sides. This will enable the cake to level up evenly during baking.

6 Bake in a preheated oven at 170°C for 1 hour or until a skewer inserted into the centre of the cake comes out clean.

Coffee Cake

Ingredients

Butter for greasing	
Butter	125 g, softened
Plain (all-purpose) flour for dusting	
Castor (superfine) sugar	125 g
Eggs	3
Self-raising flour	150 g, sifted
Fresh milk	1 Tbsp
Coffee emulco	1 tsp

Cake Tin Sizes

15 cm hexagonal cake tin

Cupcake tray with 4 cm cups

4 cm dariole tins

Method

1 Lightly grease the cake tin/cupcake moulds/dariole tins and dust with plain flour.

2 With an electric mixer, beat sugar and butter until light and fluffy.

3 Add eggs one at a time, beating well after each addition.

4 Fold in flour then combine thoroughly with milk and coffee emulco. Spoon mixture into cake tin or cupcake mould.

5 Bake in a preheated oven at 180°C. If using a cake tin, bake for 50–55 minutes or until a skewer inserted in the centre of the cake comes out clean. If using cupcake tray or dariole tins, bake for 20–25 minutes.

Swiss Roll

Ingredients

Butter for greasing	
Egg yolks	6
Castor (superfine) sugar	100 g
Egg whites	4
Plain (all-purpose) flour	75 g
Corn flour (cornstarch)	25 g
Salt	$^1/_8$ tsp

Cake Tin Size

32 x 21 cm Swiss roll tin

Method

1 Line the tin with greaseproof paper and grease well.

2 Beat egg yolks with half of the castor sugar until pale and light.

3 In another bowl, whip egg whites and remaining sugar until stiff peaks form.

4 Sift flour, corn flour and salt into egg yolk mixture. Stir well.

5 Fold egg white mixture in lightly and combine well. Level into the prepared tin.

6 Bake in a preheated oven at 220°C for 12–15 minutes or until a skewer inserted into the centre of the cake comes out clean.

7 Leave cake in tin and cover with a damp towel. Allow to cool before turning out onto a work surface.

8 Peel off greaseproof paper and spread cake with desired filling. Roll up tightly to form a Swiss roll.

Carrot Cake

Cake Tin Size

17.5 cm heart-shaped cake tin

Ingredients

Butter for greasing	
Self-raising flour	100 g
Bicarbonate of soda	1/2 tsp
Butter	100 g, softened
Soft dark brown sugar	100 g
Eggs	2
Carrots	100 g, peeled and grated
Walnuts	50 g, finely chopped
Raisins	80 g

Method

1 Line a heart-shaped cake tin with greaseproof paper and grease well. Set aside.

2 Combine flour and bicarbonate of soda and sift.

3 Cream softened butter and sugar until light and fluffy. Add one egg and beat well.

4 Mix in 2 Tbsp sifted flour and continue to beat. Add remaining egg and beat to combine.

5 Fold in remaining sifted flour, then add carrots, walnuts and raisins. Mix well. Spoon mixture into tin.

6 Bake in a preheated oven at 180°C for 40–45 minutes or until a skewer inserted into the centre of cake comes out clean.

Strawberry Cake

Cake Tin Sizes

Use 4 cylindrical cake tins:
• two 6 cm wide
• one 8 cm wide
• one 10 cm wide

Ingredients

Butter for greasing	
Plain (all-purpose) flour for dusting	
Butter	175 g, softened
Castor (superfine) sugar	175 g
Eggs	3, beaten
Self-raising flour	175 g
Baking powder	1¹⁄₂ tsp
Strawberry emulco	

Method

1 Grease the 4 cylindrical cake tins and dust with plain flour.

2 In a large bowl, combine softened butter, sugar, eggs, flour, baking powder and strawberry emulco.

3 With an electric mixer, beat well until mixture is thoroughly blended.

4 Level mixture into cake tins and fill each one until about three-quarters full.

5 Bake in a preheated oven at 180°C for 25–30 minutes or until a skewer inserted to the centre of cakes comes out clean.

Butter Icing (1) or Butter Cream

Makes 600 g

Ingredients

Butter	125 g
Icing (confectioner's) sugar	500 g
Fresh milk	2–3 Tbsp

Method

1 Cream butter until light and fluffy.

2 Add icing sugar a little at a time and beat well.

3 Mix in enough milk until a smooth spreading consistency is formed.

4 If not using immediately, keep in a tightly covered container.

Butter Icing (2)

Makes 700 g

Ingredients

Butter	250 g
Marvello or krimwell (a special type of margarine)	250 g
Icing (confectioner's) sugar	250 g
Egg whites	3
Vanilla essence	1 tsp

Method

1 Beat butter and marvello or krimwell until light and fluffy.

2 Gradually add icing sugar and continue to beat until well mixed.

3 Add in egg whites a little at a time, beating well after each addition.

4 Mix in vanilla essence.

5 If not using immediately, keep in a tightly covered container.

Chocolate Butter Icing

Makes 500 g

Ingredients

Unsalted butter	250 g
Icing (confectioner's) sugar	210 g
Milk powder	30 g
Almond essence	1/2 tsp
Dark chocolate	125 g, melted and cooled

Method

1 Beat butter until light and fluffy.

2 Sift icing sugar and milk powder together, then gradually beat into butter.

3 Add almond essence and stir well to combine.

4 Pour in melted chocolate and beat thoroughly. If using an electric mixer, ensure that the chocolate is poured into the bowl between the beater and the edge of the bowl, otherwise it will cling to the beater.

5 Keep in a covered container, if not using immediately, to avoid a crust forming on the surface.

Cocoa Butter Icing

Makes 300 g

Ingredients

Unsalted butter	60 g
Icing (confectioner's) sugar	250 g
Cocoa powder	2 Tbsp
Vanilla essence	1 tsp

Method

1 Place butter, sugar and cocoa powder into a large bowl.

2 Beat well, scraping the sides well, until a smooth spreading consistency is formed.

3 Once sugar and cocoa powder have been incorporated, beat in vanilla essence.

4 Keep icing in a covered container if not using immediately.

Vanilla Butter Icing

Makes 500 g

Ingredients

Butter	90 g
Evaporated milk	2 Tbsp
Icing (confectioner's) sugar	460 g
Vanilla essence	1 tsp

Method

1 Melt butter over a very low heat. Do not allow it to come to a boil.

2 Mix in evaporated milk and heat through for 2 minutes.

3 Stir in icing sugar then remove from heat immediately.

4 Using an electric mixer, beat mixture until light and fluffy.

5 Add in the vanilla essence and combine thoroughly.

Royal Icing

Makes 850 g

Ingredients

Egg whites	3
Lemon juice	1 tsp
Icing (confectioner's) sugar	750 g, sifted

Method

1. Place egg whites in a clean bowl. Add lemon juice and beat slightly to break up egg whites.

2. Gradually add icing sugar, beating on low speed for a few seconds after each addition. (Use the slowest speed on the electric mixer to avoid introducing too much air into the mixture.)

3. Scrape down the sides of the bowl frequently with a spatula. Continue to beat until the soft peak consistency is achieved.

Fondant or Sugarpaste (1)

Makes 500 g

Ingredients

Egg white	1
Liquid glucose	2 Tbsp
Icing (confectioner's) sugar	500 g

Method

1. Place egg white and liquid glucose in a clean bowl.

2. Sift in icing sugar and stir until mixture begins to bind together.

3. Using your fingers, bring the mixture together to form a ball.

4. Dust a work surface lightly with icing sugar and knead fondant until smooth. Adding more icing sugar if necessary. Store in an airtight container to prevent drying out.

Fondant or Sugarpaste (2)

Makes 800 g

Ingredients

Vegetable shortening	60 g
Lemon juice	2 Tbsp
Water	2 Tbsp
Icing (confectioner's) sugar	750 g

Method

1. Place shortening, lemon juice and water in a saucepan.

2. Heat gently, stirring often until shortening has melted.

3. Sift 250 g icing sugar into pan. Stir continuously over low heat.

4. Once sugar has dissolved, do not stir. As soon as mixture starts to boil, remove from heat.

5. Gradually add enough of the remaining sugar to form a soft paste. Mix until mixture is smooth.

6. Dust a work surface lightly with extra icing sugar and knead fondant until it is no longer sticky. Add more icing sugar until fondant is firm. Store in an airtight container to prevent drying out.

Marzipan or Almond Paste

Makes 480 g

Ingredients

Icing (confectioner's) sugar	100 g
Castor (superfine) sugar	100 g
Ground almonds	225 g
Lemon juice	1 tsp
Egg	1, lightly beaten

Method

1 Place the icing sugar and castor sugar into a large bowl.

2 Add almonds and lemon juice and stir thoroughly.

3 Mix in enough egg to bind the mixture into a firm paste.

4 Place almond mixture on a work surface lightly dusted with icing sugar.

5 Knead lightly until smooth. Do not over handle the paste as it may turn oily.

Coloured Desiccated Coconut or Sugar

Ingredients

Desiccated coconut/
granulated sugar

Food colouring

Method

1 Place desiccated coconut or sugar into a bowl.

2 Add a drop of food colouring at a time and mix well until desired shade is achieved.

Gelatine Icing

Makes 1 kg

Ingredients

Hot water	63 ml
Gelatine powder	1 Tbsp
Liquid glucose	125 ml
Glycerine	1 Tbsp
Vegetable shortening	2 Tbsp
Icing (confectioner's) sugar	900 g

Method

1 Pour hot water into a large pan. Sprinkle in gelatine powder and set aside for 5 minutes.

2 Place pan over low heat and stir until gelatine dissolves.

3 Combine liquid glucose, glycerine and shortening. Stir until shortening begins to melt.

4 Remove from heat immediately and continue to stir until shortening is completely melted.

5 Allow mixture to cool slightly then gradually add icing sugar, stirring well after each addition.

6 Dust a work surface lightly with icing sugar. Knead fondant, adding enough icing sugar until it is smooth and free from cracks.

Blue Piping Jelly

Ingredients

Piping jelly	4 Tbsp
Blue food colouring	

Method

1 Place piping jelly into a small bowl.

2 Add a drop of blue food colouring at a time and mix well until desired shade is achieved.

Mixing Colours

Coloured Butter Cream/Royal Icing/Fondant/Marzipan

To colour butter cream, royal icing, fondant or marzipan, add a drop of food colouring at a time and stir or knead well until the desired shade is achieved.

Prepare all the colours needed before you start on a cake and store them in small plastic airtight food bags to prevent them from drying out when not in use.

Important Notes on Colours

Primary Colours

These are red, blue and yellow. They cannot be created by mixing any other colours together.

Secondary Colours

This refers to purple, orange and purple. They are obtained by mixing equal parts of any 2 primary colours.

- Red + blue = purple
- Red + yellow = orange
- Yellow + blue = purple

Tertiary Colours

This refers to shades of all colours. Such colours can be obtained by mixing secondary and primary colours.

Hints on Mixing Colours

Be adventurous in mixing colours to try and see what you will get! Here are some suggestions on achieving commonly used colours.

- Chrome yellow = yellow + 1–2 drops of orange or red
- Lime green = green + 1–2 drops of yellow
- Sea green = green + royal blue
- Brick red = brown + red
- Orange = lemon yellow + red
- Grey = use 1–2 drops of black
- Tan = brown + 1–2 drops of yellow

Tips on Using Colouring

- Use paste or gel food colours when colouring fondant or sugarpaste.
- Apply colour in small amounts with a cocktail stick. Mix well before adding more to achieve desired shade.
- When kneading in the colours, protect your hands from staining by wearing plastic gloves.
- Some colours may fade if completed cake is exposed to direct sunlight, so try to keep cakes in a cool, shaded spot.

Equipment

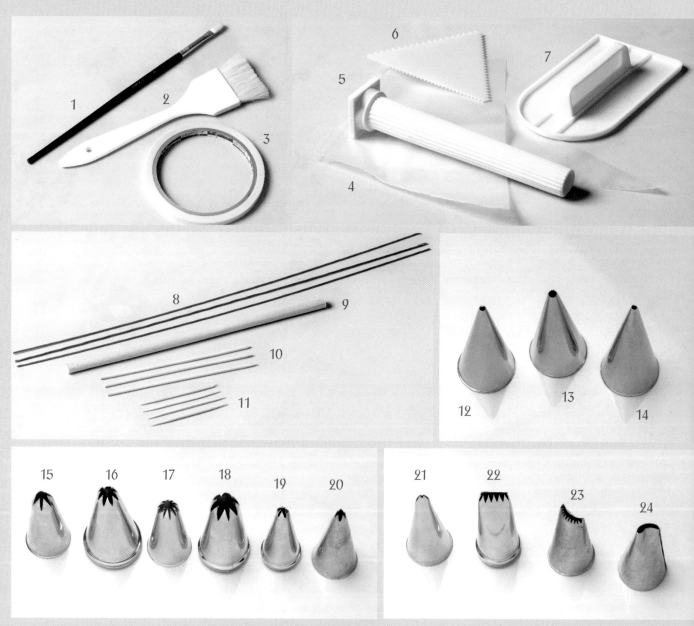

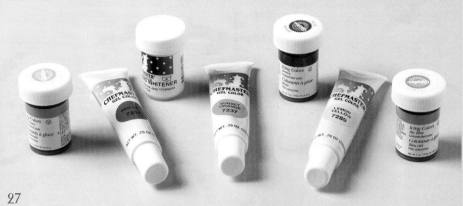

1. Fine tip paintbrush

2. Glazing brush

3. Double-sided tape

4. Piping bag

5. Long plastic dowel

6. Cake comb

7. Cake smoother

8. Green florist wires

9. Balsa wood dowel rod

10. Bamboo skewers

11. Cocktail sticks

12. Writing tip no. 2

13. Writing tip no. 4

14. Writing tip no. 1

15. Bakery crafts 131 star tip

16. Ruby FM 809 star tip

17. Bakery crafts 15 star tip

18. Ruby FM 820 star tip

19. Ruby FM 824 star tip

20. Bakery crafts 504 star tip

21. Bakery crafts 66 leaf tip

22. Ruby FM 803 ribbon tip

23. Bakery crafts 98 shell tip

24. Rutbrown 18 petal tip

25. Garrett frill cutter, fluted, round

26. Round cutter

27. Food colouring

28. Wafer flowers

29. Sugarpaste flowers

Weights and Measures

Quantities for this book are given in Metric and American (spoon) measures. Standard measurements used are: 1 tsp = 5 ml, 1 dsp = 10 ml, 1 Tbsp = 15 ml, 1 cup = 250 ml. All measures are level unless otherwise stated.

LIQUID AND VOLUME MEASURES

Metric	Imperial	American
5 ml	$^1/_6$ fl oz	1 teaspoon
10 ml	$^1/_3$ fl oz	1 dessertspoon
15 ml	$^1/_2$ fl oz	1 tablespoon
60 ml	2 fl oz	$^1/_4$ cup (4 tablespoons)
85 ml	$2^1/_2$ fl oz	$^1/_3$ cup
90 ml	3 fl oz	$^3/_8$ cup (6 tablespoons)
125 ml	4 fl oz	$^1/_2$ cup
180 ml	6 fl oz	$^3/_4$ cup
250 ml	8 fl oz	1 cup
300 ml	10 fl oz ($^1/_2$ pint)	$1^1/_4$ cups
375 ml	12 fl oz	$1^1/_2$ cups
435 ml	14 fl oz	$1^3/_4$ cups
500 ml	16 fl oz	2 cups
625 ml	20 fl oz (1 pint)	$2^1/_2$ cups
750 ml	24 fl oz ($1^1/_5$ pints)	3 cups
1 litre	32 fl oz ($1^3/_5$ pints)	4 cups
1.25 litres	40 fl oz (2 pints)	5 cups
1.5 litres	48 fl oz ($2^2/_5$ pints)	6 cups
2.5 litres	80 fl oz (4 pints)	10 cups

DRY MEASURES

Metric	Imperial
30 grams	1 ounce
45 grams	$1^1/_2$ ounces
55 grams	2 ounces
70 grams	$2^1/_2$ ounces
85 grams	3 ounces
100 grams	$3^1/_2$ ounces
110 grams	4 ounces
125 grams	$4^1/_2$ ounces
140 grams	5 ounces
280 grams	10 ounces
450 grams	16 ounces (1 pound)
500 grams	1 pound, $1^1/_2$ ounces
700 grams	$1^1/_2$ pounds
800 grams	$1^3/_4$ pounds
1 kilogram	2 pounds, 3 ounces
1.5 kilograms	3 pounds, $4^1/_2$ ounces
2 kilograms	4 pounds, 6 ounces

OVEN TEMPERATURE

	°C	°F	Gas Regulo
Very slow	120	250	1
Slow	150	300	2
Moderately slow	160	325	3
Moderate	180	350	4
Moderately hot	190/200	370/400	5/6
Hot	210/220	410/440	6/7
Very hot	230	450	8
Super hot	250/290	475/550	9/10

LENGTH

Metric	Imperial
0.5 cm	$^1/_4$ inch
1 cm	$^1/_2$ inch
1.5 cm	$^3/_4$ inch
2.5 cm	1 inch

ABBREVIATION

tsp	teaspoon
dsp	dessertspoon
Tbsp	tablespoon
g	gram
ml	millilitre